How To Grade

And Rank Every

 Basketballer

In

History

by Arthur R. Linton, B.Sc.

ISBN: 1-58112-866-5

UPUBLISH.COM
1998

www.upublish.com/books/linton.htm

This book is dedicated to the basketball industry,
to all my family, and all my friends.

Disclaimer

Although the formula was used to calculate the EFs assigned to the players and is very accurate, the author makes no warranty or representation, either expressed or implied, with respect to the usefulness of the formula or data for a particular purpose. In no case will the author, the publisher, or the distributors be liable for direct, indirect, special, incidental, or consequential damages arising out of the use or inability to use the formula or data in this book.

The exclusion of implied warranties is not permitted by some states. Therefore, the above exclusion may not apply to you. This warranty provides you with specific legal rights; there may be other rights that you may have that vary from state to state.

Table of Contents

About The Author

Arthur Linton is a retired electrical engineer. He has been at home since 1996 because of illness and has used his new "freedom" to research and develop the principles presented. He spent over a decade in engineering design and construction with an electric power company. His training and experience in project management involved the development of systems to measure human effort for numerous, diverse, tasks. He may be contacted from his web site at:

www.geocities.com/colosseum/pressbox/5326

or by e-mail at: **arlinton_98@yahoo.com**

Arthur currently lives with his wife and two daughters in Miami, Florida.

The Author's Acknowledgments

Special thanks to Trevor and Elaine Coombs, Corliss Reid, Shernette Stafford, Charles McLean, and Caswell Linton, whose encouragement and assistance helped to make this project possible.

Thanks also to my daughters Kay-Ann and Camille to my wife ,Angie, who helped with this project in one way or another. The kind words and interest of many other family members ,and of my general physician, Dr. David Nhor, helped significantly. Thanks to the basketball industry for providing such an entertaining sport and to you for your interest in this book.

Many thanks to Jeff Young and the staff of UPUBLISH.COM.

Introduction

You may have noticed that engineers and scientists make major decisions from established formulae, computer models, and other proven methods. A trip to the moon, say, involves numerous precise calculations. As an engineer, I know instinctively that to rank basketballers from fan-polls is arbitrary and will only give biased results. After viewing some team boxscores, I realized that the basketball world had done a great job at data recording. All the inputs were in place to facilitate the development of an objective, mathematical model to grade and rank the players of all times for all times, even during games. So,using principles, I developed for engineering projects, I decided to approach this situation as if my assigned project was the management of a basketball team. Quite naturally, I would need a system that allowed me to monitor both my players and my opponents. Some operations the new management information formula would allow are:

- The grading of players for each minute they played
- The ranking of players, of all decades from their performance statistics.
- Making strategic player substitutions during games
- Precise decision making when trading and acquiring players

In the final analysis my management information system(MIS) should allow me to monitor all players and tell me exactly what my team needed to do to win the championship.

The resulting formula I developed amazed me. It am confident that it can improve operations, in the front office, in the gym, and on the court, substantially.

Between 1980 and 1993, I worked as an engineer for an electric power company. One of the main principles I acquired from that experience was that human physical effort, regardless of the task at hand, was quantifiable. Once, as a substation construction engineer, I had to estimate the man-hours needed to complete each of scores of different tasks. To do that, an appreciation of the units that could measure each task was required. Sometimes new units had to be established to accurately mimic the actual work done. At one stage, during the earlier years, I routinely spent many hours, on site, monitoring workers and recording the work- progress to facilitate preparation of my weekly progress reports.

The directors, however, were not interested in the number of cables installed or the length of trench dug. They simply wanted to know the percentage of the whole job completed each week and the scheduled completion date. So, my long hours of observation and calculations were summarized by a single figure at the end of each week. I needed to be thoroughly abreast of the details, however, to give realistic figures which often were passed on to the public relations department. Those figures not only gave information on the rate at which the project was proceeding but also told management whether one understood the job and if one was to be considered for promotions.

The many variables used to define a basketballer's performance are really fine details or raw data. To plan, organize, manage, and control basketball operations, a new composite unit is needed. Such a unit will allow the administrators the ease of grading and ranking players, choosing MVPs, making trades and acquisitions, and many other tasks, without being swamped with the fine details. The boxscores and other statistics are mainly needed by players, coaches, enthusiasts, commentators, and fans. Administrators need a player's statistics for their personal knowledge, in most cases, and not for decision-making. With one carefully designed index per player, they should be able to perform their functions effectively.

Presently, many administrative decisions are being done by arbitrary means, such as votes and fan-polls. While these means are quite useful in making decisions involving abstract features, such as beauty and popularity, they are unsuitable for making decisions about physical effort. In sports, athletes do actual work. From basic physics, power is defined as : the rate at which work is done. So, if we identify all the tasks a player performs for a particular sport and assign points to each, the total number of points accumulated by each player may be tabulated at the end of any time-period. The points would give a measure of the work done by the athlete. By dividing the "work done" by the time the player took to do it, one could mathematically represent the player's " power". Such a unit would allow the performances of all players of a particular sport to be evaluated on an equal basis, regardless of their era, sex, or age.

The values obtained by this method allow comparisons to be made mathematically thus enabling the basketball world the ability to make operational decisions previously either unconsidered or decided by polls. Now, a basketballer's performance will have units of points- per-minute which is similar to watts for generators or horsepower for machines.

In this book, I will show you how to develop a formula for a new unit I called the **Effectiveness Factor (EF)**. Later, this formula will be further manipulated to reveal useful coaching rules. Some of the data and new methods now made possible by this mathematical model will also be presented. EF provides all the feedback needed to control basketball operations involving players and administrators. I am specially encouraged to succeed as I know many people need this formula.

I bought a magazine recently in which the very editor stated: "Given the impossibility of fairly comparing players of different eras, our plan was to compare players to playersof their own era to see how they distinguished themselves from their contemporaries." While this may be good enough for some analysts , it is unfair to those players who were runners-up in previous decades but undoubtedly could win championships in other generations.

PART I

A

New

Standard

For

Basketballers

CHAPTER ONE

Performance Units And Standards In Athletics

Some of the units used to measure performance in sports are:

- **time;** hobsledding, racing

- **height;** high- jump

- **length;** long- jump

- **distance;** javelin, shot putt

- **points;** boxing, tennis, most team sports

- **amount:** weight- lifting

- **EF(evaluated points-per-minute) is a new unit the author developed for basketball.**

Usually athletic achievement can be determined by monitoring the time each athlete took to cover a common distance, the distance by which a common object was displaced (time =0), or the points accumulated in a common time, in both competitive and non-competitive cases of some group and individual sports.

Weight- lifting may be interpreted to be measured in units of points-per-kilogram lifted.

One common unit to which all others may be converted is man-hours. In some cases to complete a task, a great number of sub-tasks must done initially. Sometimes the only data available is that " it took five men 10 days

(80 hours) to do that task on the previous project." So we know that the activity would take approximately 400 (5 x 80) man-hours.

Naturally, you may be wondering why this information is even considered. However, if one can approximate the number of man-hours needed for a project, one can estimate the labor costs involved and give an estimated completion time. The directors usually wanted these estimates before approving any funds for any project. An engineer's annual appraisal was also tied to his or her ability to have projects completed on time and within budget.

CHAPTER TWO

A New Unit Needed For Basketball

As stated previously, the basketball industry, needs a new unit that will isolate administrators from the details regularly needed by players and coaches. In the final analysis, games are usually won by the team that scores the greater number of points for that game. The data on assists, steals, rebounds, blocks, and so on, are good for commentaries and discussions, but games are won by points scored. If all the performance units are assumed to be contributors to points, the total evaluated points contributed by each player can be obtained at any time. Each player can be ranked according to the rate at which he or she accumulates evaluated points. Evaluated points allow the work of the players to be measured on an equal basis, regardless of their game positions. Point-guards are expected to lead most of their other team members in , steals, and assists. However, a good center will be correspondingly effective in the categories of blocking and rebounding.

Some players are excellent in that, although they sit on the bench for most of a game, they contribute at a high rate whenever they are injected into the game.

CHAPTER THREE

Effectiveness Factor (EF)

With a consistent unit and relative comparisons, great results are possible. A player's performance may be defined as follows:

$$EF = (2AST + PTS + 0.4R + 0.4STL + 2BLK - 0.6TO)/TMP$$

where:

- **EF = effectiveness factor**
- **STL = total steals**
- **TO   = total turnovers**
- **AST = total assists**
- **BLK = total blocks**
- **PTS = total points scored**
- **TMP = total minutes played**
- **R   = total rebounds**

In this formula, the weighting factors used are subjective. This mathematical model declares that one BLK is as important as scoring a two-pointer. Quite naturally, various coaches will have different views, depending on the player -qualities they want to highlight. An Effectiveness Factor measuring a player's average performance over any duration can be calculated: game, regular season, post season, tournament, career, etc. A player's EF is expected to fluctuate above and below his or her seasonal average and may vary significantly from game to game.

While it may be used to determine a player's expected performance, his or her actual output for a particular game can not be predicted. Also, with training, players may improve their EFs as the season progresses. Controlling ones EF may be necessary in some cases.

Players with higher EFs are not necessarily better than low EF players since EF has both offensive and a defensive components. A center with an EF of 0.500 may be more important to a team's success than a forward with an EF of 0.600.
The EF is a measure of a player's contribution for each minute he or she plays. Some players with low EFs, specialize in certain areas such as

rebounding- Dennis Rodman. Outstanding players will have an average EF of near one regardless of how much time is spent on the court. Rodman's EF is usually about 0.500 as he concentrates mostly on defense. So, his EF is largely a measure of his defensive capabilities and not his total game potential.

Checking The Calculations

$$EF = (2AST+PTS+0.4R+0.4STL + 2BLK - 0.6TO)/TMP$$

For Tim Hardaway (1997-98 Regular Season),

STL= 136 : BLK=16: TO=224: AST=672: R=299 :PTS=1528: TGP=81: TMP=3031:

These figures give a value of:

$$EF\text{-Tim Hardaway} = (2 \times 672 + 1528 + 0.4 \times 299 + 0.4 \times 136 + 2 \times 16 - 0.6 \times 224)/3031$$
$$= (1344 + 1528 + 119.6 + 54.4 + 32 - 134.4)/3031$$

$$= 0.97 \text{ pt/minute}$$

All the EFs were calculated with a spreadsheet. So, if one calculation is correct, all the others should also be correct, once the correct data was inputted, as the same formula was used in each case and the calculations done by the computer.

The above calculation was the only one done manually and just for confirmation that the formula was correctly represented on the spreadsheet.

It must be noted that if the Effectiveness Factor was based on different TMPs(total minutes played), the values obtained would vary. The average EF for a player will lessen as that player nears retirement. The average basketballer should expect to have career Efs ranging from 0.400 - 0.600, say .

7

After finding EFs for all the WNBA and NBA players for 1997 and some of the Hall Of Famers, the following pattern was noticed:

EF Range	Comments
0.000-0.599	Average Players
0.600-0.799	Good Players
0.800-0.899	Very Good
0.900-0.999	Stars
1.000-1.499	Superstars
1.500-1.599	Exceptional
1.600-1.799	Outstanding
1.800-1.999	Best Ever

Average EFs obtained for various categories in the NBA 1997-98 playoffs were:

Guards/Forwards

1	Eddie Jones	0.752
2	Glen Rice	0.703
3	N. Mcmillan	0.582
4	Dell Curry	0.517
5	Dale Ellis	0.435
6	W. Person	0.418
7	Majerle	0.397
8	Buechler	0.382
9	A. Bowie	0.278
10	Askins	0.183

Avg G/F= 0.465

Guards

1	Jordan	1.044
2	Tim Hardaway	0.924
3	Charlie. Ward	0.802
4	John Starks	0.746
5	Allan Houston	0.710
6	Murdock	0.702
7	Harper-Chicago	0.608
8	V. Lenard	0.527
9	Brown-Chicago	0.489
10	Steve Kerr	0.455

Avg G= 0.701

Forwards/Guards

1	Pippen	0.821
2	Kukoc	0.676
3	Burrell	0.674
4	Mario Ellie	0.383

Avg F/G= 0.639

Forwards/Centers

1	O. Harrington*	0.904
2	Tim Duncan	0.803
3	A. Mcdyess	0.763
4	Elden Campbell	0.729
5	Mark Bryant	0.611
6	Kevin Willis	0.574
7	S. Perkiness	0.505
8	Brad Lohaus	0.320
9	Matt Geiger	0.273

Avg F/C= 0.609

Forwards

1	L. Johnson	0.646
2	T. Cummings	0.513

3	M. Strickland	0.493
4	Dennis Rodman	0.488
5	Jamal Mashburn	0.473
6	Terry Mills	0.473
7	C. Oakley	0.443
8	P.J. Brown	0.423
9	M. Conlon	0.370
10	Dickey Simpkins	0.352

Avg F= 0.467

Centers/Forwards

1	Antoine Carr	0.589
2	Rasheed Wallace	0.589
3	John Williams	0.424
4	V. Potapenko	0.403

Avg C/F 0.501

Centers

1	Shaquille Oneal	1.270
2	H. Olajuwon	0.956
3	David Robinson	0.952
4	Alonzo Mourning	0.883
5	Rik Smits	0.849
6	Kelvin Cato	0.814
7	Arvydas Sabonis	0.768
8	Luc Longley	0.755
9	Greg Anderson	0.700
10	Vlade Divac	0.684

Avg C= 0.863

* In this case the player only played for a very short time.

Part II

Ranking

Lists

CHAPTER FOUR

Using EF To Evaluate And Grade Players

A further step may be taken and grades will be systematically assigned to the EF ranges as follows:

Grade	EF Range
A9	1.900-1.999
A8	1.800-1.899
A7	1.700-1.799
A6	1.600-1.699
A5	1.500-1.599
A4	1.400-1.499
A3	1.300-1.399
A2	1.200-1.299
A1	1.100-1.199
A0	1.000-1.099
B9	0.900-0.999
B8	0.800-0.899
B7	0.700-0.799
B6	0.600-0.699
B5	0.500-0.599
B4	0.400-0.499
B3	0.300-0.399
B2	0.200-0.299
B1	0.100-0.199
B0	0.000-0.099

Using the above system, every player can be graded and his level of performance preserved for future generations. We would all know that George Mikan of the 1949-50 Minnesota Lakers was a grade A7 center. Players could be graded as follows:

Max Zaslofsky	A5
Magic Johnson (86-87)	A4
Michael Olowokandi	A0
Cynthia Cooper (97-98)	B9

The talent scouts would simply need to know that Michael Olowokandi was a grade A0 center to confirm that choosing him as the NBA 1998 number one draft pick was a good decision. Such a system will ensure that sound, objective, records are kept over all generations. You may have noticed that only two main grades were used: A, and B. So far no one in history has gotten higher than an A9. The star players are usually graded B8 and higher.

CHAPTER FIVE

Best Male Performers Of All-Times

List prepared by: Arthur Linton

Date: September 1998

Rank	Player	EF
01	Joe Fulks	1.958
02	*George Mikan(career)	1.792
03	Max Zaslofsky	1.556
04	*Magic Johnson(86-87)	1.443
05	*Michael Jordan(88-89)	1.357
06	*John Stockton(89-90)	1.308
07	*Shaquille Oneal(97-98)	1.270
08	*David Robinson(93-94)	1.257
09	Gail Goodrich(71-72)	1.219
10	*Jerry West(71-72)	1.214
	*Olajuwon(92-93)	1.201
	*Patrick Ewing(89-90)	1.186
	*Kareem. Abdul Jabbar(79-80)	1.184
	* Bob Cousy(59-60)	1.169
	Tim Hardaway(90-91)	1.154
	*Karl Malone(96-97)	1.136
	*Robert Parish(80-81)	1.136
	*Oscar Robertson	1.130
	*Charles Barkley(90-91)	1.120
	Rod Stkickland(94-95)	1.116
	Sam Cassell(97-98)	1.096
	Kevin Johnson(93-94)	1.095
	*Wilt Chamberlain(66-67)	1.086
	Penny Hardaway(95-96)	1.073
	George Gervin	1.067
	*Larry Bird	1.065
	*Julius Erving(82-83)	1.062
	Grant Hill(96-97)	1.054
	Allen Iverson(96-97)	1.037
	Alonzo Mourning(93-94)	1.036

*Elgin Baylor	1.033
*Rick Barry	1.025
*Isaiah Thomas(88-89)	1.021
Jim Pollard	1.021
M. Olowokandi(97-98)	1.018
*Bob Petit	1.006
*Moses Malone(82-83)	1.005
*Paul Arizin	1.004
*Walt Frazier(69-70)	1.004
Andrew Toney(82-83)	1.004
*Nate "Tiny" Archibald	0.997
*Pete Maravich	0.994
Ed Macauley(49-59)	0.994
*Dolph Schayes	0.988
Baylok(93-94)	0.983
*Scottie Pippen 1995-96	0.980
Gary Payton(1997-98)	0.969
*Billy Cunningham	0.966
*Kevin McHale(85-86)	0.964
Tom Heinsohn(59-60)	0.946
Dave Bing	0.942
Bobby Wanzer	0.938
Maurice Cheeks(82-83)	0.931
Wilkins(93-94)	0.931
Sam Jones(64-65)	0.929
Grant Hill(97-98)	0.928
Arnie Risen(46-58)	0.926
Clyde Drexler(93-94)	0.920
Bill Sharman(59-60)	0.920
John Starks(93-94)	0.919
Bogues(93-94)	0.918
Marbury(97-98)	0.916
Wilkins(93-94)	0.916
Troy Hudson	0.913
Chris Webber	0.909
John Havlicek	0.908
Norm Nixon(79-80)	0.902
Bill Walton(85-86)	0.893
Sam Jones	0.884
Toni Kukoc 1995-96	0.876
James Worthy(86-87)	0.866
Dennis Johnson(85-86)	0.859
Dave Cowens	0.836
Bill Russell(59-60)	0.831
Hal Greer(66-67)	0.823

Willis Reed(69-70)	0.818
Tim Duncan	0.803
James Worthy	0.792
Bob Dandridge(70-71)	0.789
Jerry Lucas	0.770
Bill Bradley(69-70)	0.764
Bobby Jones(82-83)	0.745
Dave DeBusschere	0.740
Pat Riley(71-72)	0.702
Jim McMillian(71-72)	0.698

*Thirty-one of the first 50 players from the above list are on the NBA's top 50 list. The NBA has been 62% accurate using subjective means.The above list accurately includes some current players. The nuance of true greatness cannot be easily distinguished by the human observer. Also, it is quite natural for great players among us to be overlooked by their peers, just as Fulks was ignored by many. So, to set the records straight, a list of current (1998) players who gave a top 50 performances, at some point in their career is:

- Michael Jordon
- John Stockton
- Shaquille Oneal
- David Robinson
- Hakeem Olajuwon
- Patrick Ewing
- Tim Hardaway
- Karl Malone
- Charles Barkley
- Rod Strickland
- Sam Cassell
- Kevin Johnson
- Penny Hardaway
- Grant Hill
- Allen Iverson
- Alonzo Mourning
- Michael Olowokandi
- Mookie Baylock
- Scottie Pippen
- Gary Payton

The players are listed in order of their "greatness." That is, the best EF they have attained thus far. So, 40% of the 50 best performances ever are from current players. Every era has great players.

One of the major advantages of using EF to rank players is that the list remains dynamic and every living player has the same opportunity to become the greatest. It is unfair for players to perform in an atmosphere in which the top 50 players of all time are already fixed. No one has a monopoly on geatness. Any player can become the best. That status is largely a function of skill, dedication, and determination.

You may maintain a current list yourself. Simply calculate the EF of the best basketballers and insert them in order of greatness as the years progress. Also, you may establish and maintain a ranking list of players in any league and for any team you desire.

This method should be useful for coaches of national teams preparing for, say, the Olympics. The players may be ranked after each practice, even during practice players can be told their overall EF level or for any duration the coach wants to monitor. Players may be monitored for an entire game and a graph of EF against time-played plotted.. Coaches should be aware of how their players' EFs vary as their playing time is increased.

Ideally, I would have liked to have evaluated all the players listed in the *Official NBA Directory* but that task was unnecessary for this book. I plan to do that in the future and maintain a list of all the players in NBA history. Readers are encouraged to use the formula to establish and maintain lists of their own. You have my permission to publish your lists as you desire.

CHAPTER SIX

List Of Best 1997-98 NBA Performers

Some of the better 1997-98 regular season performances were evaluated as follows:

Shaquille Oneal	1.128
Karl Malone	1.051
David Robinson	1.046
Sam Cassell	1.034
John Stockton	1.011
Rod Strickland	1.011
Michael Jordan	0.990
Tim Hardaway	0.971
Gary Payton	0.969
Terrell Brandon	0.940
Grant Hill	0.928
P. Ewing	0.918
S. Marbury	0.916
Troy Hudson	0.913
Chris Webber	0.909
Scottie Pippen	0.904
Allen Iverson	0.901
Clyde Drexler	0.894
T. Edney	0.889
Mark Jackson	0.889
Nick Van Exel	0.885
Tim Duncan	0.885
God Shammgod	0.877
Mitch Richmond	0.866
B. Knight	0.860
Kevin Garnett	0.859
Willie Burton	0.856
Damon Stoudamire	0.856
S. Abdur-rahim	0.853
Hakeem Olajuwon	0.852
Arvydas Sabonis	0.843

Kobe Bryant	0.841
Joe Stephens	0.838
Jason Kidd	0.836
A. Walker	0.833
G. Anthony	0.833
Alonzo Mourning	0.831
Rik Smits	0.831
D. Baros	0.829
Gugiiotta	0.823
Mark Price	0.823
Chet Walker	0.820
M. Williams	0.817
Latrell Sprewell	0.816
Horacio Llamas	0.814
Michael Finley	0.804
Danny Manning	0.804
Gary Grant	0.804
William Cunningham	0.800
Shawn Bradley	0.795
Charles Barkley	0.795
Shawn Kemp	0.793
Mario Bennet	0.792
Wali Jones	0.792
Marcus Camby	0.789
Chris Whitney	0.789
Jeff Hornacek	0.789
Penny Hardaway	0.786
Toni Kukoc	0.784
Kenny Anderson	0.784
Jimmy Oliver	0.780
A. Mcdyess	0.779
Howard Eisley	0.778
Kevin Johnson	0.772
Sherman Douglas	0.766
David Wesley	0.765
D. Schrempf	0.765
J. Cotton	0.764
D. Armstrong	0.763
Vin Baker	0.762
Derrick Coleman	0.761
Vlade Divac	0.760
Matt Geiger	0.756
Cedric Ceballos	0.754
Steve Smith	0.754
Chris Crawford	0.752

Glen Robinson	0.750
N. Anderson	0.747
Z. Ilgauskas	0.745
Mookie Baylock	0.742
E. Williams	0.742
Avery Johnson	0.740
C. Ward	0.738
B. Jackson	0.734
Elden Campbell	0.730
G. Alexander	0.730
J. Stackhouse	0.730
C. Williamson	0.727
Tracy Mcgrady	0.727
Byrant Reeves	0.726
Travis Best	0.726
Ray Allen	0.726
Murdock	0.726
Christian Laettner	0.725
Dikembe Mutombo	0.721
Issac Austin	0.721
Isaiah Rider	0.720
James Collins	0.713
Reggie Miller	0.712
George Lynch	0.707
K. Edwards	0.706
John Starks	0.706
Maurice Taylor	0.706
Tony Delk	0.703
Doug Christie	0.702
Allan Houston	0.701
Tom Chambers	0.700
D. Anderson	0.697
Glen Rice	0.697
Blue Edwards	0.697
Chauncey Billups	0.696
John Wallace	0.695
Booth	0.694
Luc Longley	0.693
B. Thompson	0.691
B.J. Armstrong	0.690
Day	0.687
Donyell Marshall	0.685
Rodney Rogers	0.685
Kevin Willis	0.684

P. Lauderdale	0.682
James Robinson	0.681
L. Ellis	0.678
O. Polynice	0.677
Keith Van Horn	0.676
Chris Gatling	0.673
Jim Jackson	0.673
Bobby Hurley	0.672
Kerry Kittles	0.671
Brian Williams	0.670
Marty Conlon	0.667
Joe Smith	0.667
Chris Mullin	0.663
M. Abdul-rauf	0.663
Bob Sura	0.661
L. Funderburke	0.659
Tyrone Bogues	0.657
Walt Williams	0.649
T. Knight	0.645
Kurt Thomas	0.644
Steve Henson	0.640
Jearald Honeycutt	0.634
Joe Dumars	0.628
Khalid Reeves	0.628
Lucious Jackson	0.626
Armon Gilliam	0.621
Monty Williams	0.544

Pippen, Hardaway, Mourning, and Duncan are players whose effort and intensity are well known (1997-98). As the EF assumes that all the players are performing in the same game, The best player up to 1998 is adjudged to be Joe Fulks. Michael Jordan is the best player of the 90s.

CHAPTER SEVEN

List Of Best 1997 WNBA Performers

The best WNBA EFs for the 1997 season were:

Cooper	0.914	Comets
Leslie	0.851	Sparks
Bolton-Holifield	0.747	Monarchs
Bullett	0.744	Sting
Stinson	0.741	Sting
Swoopes	0.716	Comets
Mapp	0.714	Sting
Toler	0.714	Sparks
Branova	0.703	Starzz
Hopson-Shelton	0.662	Sting
Palmer	0.659	Starzz
Fijalkowski	0.659	Rockers
Hampton	0.658	Liberty
Timms	0.648	Mercury
Pettis	0.648	Mercury
Haixia	0.645	Sparks
Witherspoon	0.641	Liberty
Dixon	0.639	Sparks
Wicks	0.635	Liberty
Lobo	0.633	Liberty
Gillom	0.632	Mercury
Byears	0.623	Monarchs
Edwards	0.615	Rockers
Weatherspoon	0.615	Liberty
Williams	0.614	Starzz
Askamp	0.608	Mercury
Braxton	0.607	Rockers
Mabika	0.605	Sparks
Thompson	0.604	Comets
Maxwell	0.600	Rockers
Nemcova	0.579	Rockers
Gordon	0.570	Monarchs

Burge	0.562	Sparks
Brown	0.559	Rockers
Woodard	0.554	Rockers
Head	0.544	Starzz
Foster	0.544	Mercury
Arcain	0.541	Comets
Williams	0.536	Mercury
McGee	0.533	Monarchs
Hicks	0.522	Starzz
Perrot	0.520	Comets
Johnson	0.519	Liberty
Burgess	0.515	Sparks
Lieberman-Cline	0.514	Mercury
Suber	0.506	Sting
Jones	0.500	Rockers
Congreaves	0.486	Sting
Trice	0.479	Liberty
Reiss	0.478	Starzz
Jackson	0.472	Mercury
Booker	0.471	Starzz
Manning	0.468	Sting
Harris	0.466	Comets
Wideman	0.464	Sparks
Nicholson	0.459	Rockers
Blades	0.457	Liberty
Tremitiere	0.455	Monarchs
Charles	0.435	Sparks
Webb	0.431	Mercury
Colleton	0.426	Sparks
Hardmon	0.414	Starzz
Abraham	0.413	Monarchs
Moore	0.412	Sting
Levesque	0.401	Sting
Yasen	0.391	Monarchs
Ford	0.388	Liberty
Carter	0.385	Starzz
Crumpton-Moorer	0.382	Liberty
Viglione	0.367	Monarchs
Jackson	0.356	Comets
Ambers	0.351	Mercury
Johnson	0.348	Rockers
Guyton	0.346	Comets
Woosley	0.344	Comets
Hagiwara	0.337	Mercury
Savasta	0.321	Monarchs

Artis	0.315	Sting
Graves	0.312	Monarchs
Koss	0.297	Starzz
Vukadinovic	0.286	Sting
Boucek	0.261	Rockers
Moore	0.209	Comets
Gessig	-0.050	Sparks

As the EF places all players simultaneously on the same court, it is quite clear that the top WNBA basketballers would do well even in the NBA. An EF of 0.914 places Cynthia Cooper in a class by herself. The second best EF was a 0.851 from Leslie of the Los Angeles Sparks.

CHAPTER EIGHT

Past Greats And Great Prospects

Joe Fulks

After weeks of research, I came to the conclusion that Mikan was the most effective player ever and that his career EF would remain the bast for all time. Then, I decided to evaluate all the champions listed in the *World Almanac* . I noticed that Joe Fulks won the first championship and since that time I became very interested in his career statistics. One evening while on the way to the movies, my wife and daughters waited on me while I rushed to the Art and Recreation section of the Miami-Dade Main library, and noted Joe Fulks's statistics from the *Official NBA Encyclopedia*. It took me less than five minutes as I knew, from previous visits, the very shelf where basketball books were located. As soon as I saw his TMP and his corresponding PTS, I knew that Joe Fulks was an extraordinary player. So, when I rejoined my family afterwards, I immediately relayed to my wife that Joe Fulks would definitely be one of the top ten players of all-times. I carefully pocketed by prized information and we went on to the movies.

After a long evening, I finally got back to my computer, opened my spreadsheet, and entered the data. To my great surprise, his EF was number one, much higher than Mikan's. This seemed improbable, so many rechecks were done until I had to agree that Joe Fulks was the most effective basketballer in history. Now, in retrospect, it seems logical that only the very best could dare win a championship series in days of Mikan.
Joe Fulks was born in 1921 and died in 1976. He was a forward who managed to score 63 points in one game at a time when teams were averaging 60-70 points. He played in the BAA and became the best offensive player of his day.

Fulks helped develop the high scoring offensive game we know today. He was inducted into the Hall of Fame in 1977.
It seems impossible that someone could play with alost twice the intensity of the 97-98 regular season effort of Michael Jordan, but Fulks was such a player.

I searched the Internet for information on Joe Fulks and found an interesting article at :
http://www.polydor.com/mercury/artists/nba/early_years.html

A section of the article entitled *The Early Years 1946-1955* stated :

"Prior to the 1949-50 season, the National Basketball Association of America absorbed six teams from the National Basketball League and was renamed the National Basketball Association. While Mikan dominated the league, other fine players such as Dolph Schayes of Syracuse, Joe Fulks of Philadelphia, Arnie Risen and Bob Davies of Rochester and Ed Macauley of Boston and St. Louis were entertaining the fans and increasing the popularity of the game throughout the country."

Other data gathered from the Internet regarding this great player suggest that Fulks was extremely underestimated in his era and his absence from the NBA List Of 50 Greatest Players is strong evidence that his contribution to the game is still not fully appreciated. Here are some of the information written about Fulks:

- "Philadelphia's star scorer, Joe Fulks, plled in $8,000 for his league-leading 23.2 points a game."
- "Joe Fulks is credited with bringing the jump shot to the NBA...."

" Fulks was the first jump shooter. 'The league tried to make him special,'Rosenstein said.'Come close to him and it was a foul. He wasn't that great. ' "

The statistics show that some players, who never won a scoring title or a championship, have been ranked higher than Joe Fulks. This verifies that subjective comparisons in basketball give flawed, biased, results. Perhaps Joe Fulks was not popular but he was the best per- minute contributer ever. The NBA has made a big mistake by not giving him the rank and respect he truly deserves.

The Mikan Era

With an EF of 1 .792 Mikan stands out as one of the greatest players of this century, ranking second to Joe Fulks. This comes as a surprise as most of us. When Mikan's EF was first calculated, the author thought that 1.792 was incorrect and rechecked the value several times. Was this man for real? This question was answered after a trip to the Intment. George Mikan was indeed a great basketballer. Here is some of the data found on this great player:

He was born on June 18, 1924 in Joliet, Ill., and was elected to the Hall of Fame in 1959 (the year I was born). Mikan was 6-10, the first superstar and dominant big man in professional basketball. In 1944 the goaltending rule was instituted by the NCAA as Mikan swatted away too many shots. This did not prevent him from becoming an All-American from 1944-46. He was the best scorer in 1945 and 1946 and with 120 points in three games took Depaul to the 1945 NIT championship. He was voted the greatest player in the first half-century by the *Associated Press.* He won seven pro titles during his career. Playing for the Minneapolis Lakers, he led the NBA in scoring four times (1949-52), played in the first four NBA All-Star Games (MVP 1953), and led the league in rebounding twice (1952, 1953). Mikan served as commissioner of the American Basketball Association (ABA) until 1975.

The average EFs suggest that Mikan played with twice the intensity and skill of ,say, Clyde Drexler or Alonzo Mourning and was even better than Michael Jordan and Dennis Rodman together. He, however, was a little less efficient than the Jordan-Pippen or the Stockton-Malone duos but could single handedly challenge them, effectively, in any game. Mikan was a special player, the second best thus far. The feats of this man were amazing during his career and, in comparison to 1998, are still outstanding. However, such a great payer could have been easily overlooked if the statistics were not objectively studied. We need to minimize our tendency to choose the "greatest" players only from those with whom we are familiar. In another half -century, Shaquille Oneal, Magic Johnson, Michael Jordan, and all the other great players of the 90's will be forgotten and a new list of The Top 50 Greatest Players of all time might be necessary. If, however, quantitative means such as the EF measurement in this book are used to evaluate performance, the achievements of the truly great players will never be overlooked even after centuries have elapsed.

Max Zaslofsky

This player was discovered late in the study ,along with Joe Fulks. No player got a grade A5 rating until Zaslofsky. He was considered the top guard in the 1940s. His Knicks team made it to the finals three times 1951-53 but lost to the Mikan-led Minneapolis Lakers on each occasion. Max lived from 1926 to 1985 and led the NBA in scoring in 1948.

Unfortunately, this great player was overshadowed by Mikan for most of his career. One cannot help remembering Karl Malone and Charles Barkley when one thinks of Max Zaslofsky.

Michael Olowokandi

Michael Olowokandi was the first pick of the 1998 draft. No one knows
what he will achieve as a pro. He was included to measure the level
at which he is expected to perform in the NBA. His EF was obtained
from his Pacific Tigers Team Statistics for 33 games and from the value
1.018, obtained, he is expected to perform as well as Isaiah Thomas.
With training and dedication he may well be a future great.

While at Pacific, Olowokandi averaged 22.2 points per game. The next
highest points per game average on that team was 11.7 from
Adam Jacobsen who had an EF of 0.629.

CHAPTER NINE

Ring Count

Year 19–	Winner
47	Joe Fulks
48	Reggie Hermsen
49	Mikan
50	Mikan
51	Bobby Wanzer
52	Mikan
53	Mikan
54	Mikan
55	George King
56	Petit/Arzin
57	Russell/Cousy/Sharman
58	St. Louis Team
59	Russell/Cousy/Sharman
60	Russell/Cousy/Sharman
61	Russell/Cousy/Sharman
62	Russell/Cousy
63	Russell/Cousy
64	Bill Russell
65	Bill Russell
66	Bill Russell
67	Wilt Chamberlain
68	Bill Russell
69	Bill Russell
70	DeBusschere/ W. Reid
71	Kareem/Robertson
72	Chamberlain/ West
73	Earl Munroe
74	Havilicek/Cowens
75	Rick Barry
76	Havlicek
77	Bill Walton
78	Unseld/Hayes
79	Seattle Team
80	Magic/Kareem
81	Parish/Bird
82	Magic/Kareem

83	Moses Malone
84	Parish/Bird
85	Magic/Kareem
86	Parish/Bird
87	Magic/Kareem
88	Magic/Kareem
89	Isiah Thomas
90	Isiah Thomas
91	Jordan/Pippen
92	Jordan/Pippen
93	Jordan/Pippen
94	Olajuwon/Cassell
95	Olajuwon/Drexler
96	Jordan/Pippen
97	Jordan/Pippen
98	Jordan/Pippen

Bill Russell won 11 championships but got a low ranking because he was mostly defensive and did not contribute very much to his team's offense.

Part III

Analyzing

Games

CHAPTER TEN

Evaluating Games and Individuals Of The NBA 1997-98 Playoffs

This is no fluke, analysis by EFs works. Coaches have the choice of managing by their "gut feelings" and other subjective means or managing by developing and using sound scientific systems based on the facts offered by the statistics. The author has successfully used similar methods to manage very large projects on which non-scientific methods were unacceptable.

Analyzing some of the games and series of the NBA 1997-98 season should give interesting results. Some of these analyses will now be done.

Game 1 of 5 - Miami Heat/New York Knicks Series- 1997-98 Playoffs

Final score: Miami 94, Knicks 79

Knicks :

	Game EF	Regular Season
Oakley	0.525	0.519
Johnson	0.714	0.627
Mills	0.207	0.559
Houston	0.445	0.701
Ward	0.486	0.738
Starks	0.684	0.706
Childs	0.433	0.627

Heat EFs:

P J Brown	0.438	0.563
Mourning	0.791	0.831
Hardaway	0.771	0.971
Majerle	0.321	0.497
Lenard	0.444	0.566

Murdock	0.620	0.726
Mashburn	0.339	0.614
Askins	0.000	0.336
Causwell	0.000	0.509

Comments On Game 1:

The Knicks center, Patrick Ewing, 0.918, did not play in the series because of an injury.

No Knicks player was outstanding in the first game, with the exception of Larry Johnson who increased his effort by 14% over is regular season average.

The Heat's key players were below their best but the performances by Mourning and Hardaway were enough to give them victory.

Game 2 of 5 - Miami Heat/New York Knicks Series (1997-98)

Final score: **Knicks 96 Miami 86**

Knicks EFs:

Johnson	0.629
Oakley	0.422
Mills	0.238
Houston	0.895
Ward	0.785
Starks	0.890
Cummings	0.496
Childs	0.555

Heat EFs:

Brown	0.288
Mourning	1.031
Hardaway	0.682
Lenard	0.644
Majerle	0.325
Askins	0.238
Murdock	0.786
Mashburn	0.400

Comments On Game 2:

The Knicks, Larry Johnson had an average performance but Allan Houston, Ward, Cummings, Starks, and Childs were altogether too much for a brilliant 1.031 from Alonzo Mourning. Hardaway was kept way below his peak in this match.

Game 4 of 5 - Miami Heat/New York Knicks Series(1997-98)

Final score: Knicks 90, Heat 85

Heat EFs:

Brown	0.309
Mashburn	0.255
Mourning	0.847
Hardaway	1.145
Lenard	0.176
Murdock	0.504
Conlon	0.262
Askins	0.333
Strickland	0.000

Knicks EFs:

Johnson	0.711
Oakley	0.560
Dudley	0.463
Houston	0.668
Ward	0.820
Starks	0.631
Childs	0.653
Mills	0.455
Cummings	0.257
Bowie	0.000

Comments On Game 4:

Both Hardaway and Mourning gave above average performances. An EF of 1.145 by Hardaway was one of the best efforts for the 1997-98 season. However, almost all the other Heat players gave performances below their average. With a good effort from Ward and average showings from the others, the Knicks won.

Final score: Kicks 98 Miami 81

Knicks:

Oakley	0.542
Cummings	0.421
Houston	0.790
Starks	0.837
Ward	1.333
B. Williams	0.680
Childs	0.218
Bowie	0.292

Heat:

P. J. Brown	0.485
Mashburn	0.644
Causwell	0.160
Hardaway	0.804
Lenard	0.324
Murdock	0.520
Strickland	0.575
Mills	0.733
Conlon	0.400

Comments On Game 5:

Mourning and Larry Johnson were both suspended from this match. Ward had a magnificent, 1.333, game, Starks was great, and Houston and Oakley were above their averages. The Heat's Hardaway was good but well below his full potential. With this win the Knicks won the series.

Utah 88, Chicago 85

Bulls:

		Regular Season EF
Pippen	0.536	0.904
Kukoc	0.439	0.748
Longley	0.507	0.693
Jordan	0.830	0.990
Harper	0.367	0.633
Simpkins	0.029	0.515
Burrell	0.800	0.636
Beuchler	0.000	0.577
Rodman	0.205	0.449
Brown	-0.400	0.560
Kerr	0.348	0.539

Utah:

Russell	0.458	0.506
Malone	0.702	1.051
Foster	0.213	0.466
Hornacek	0.309	0.789
Stockton	1.137	1.011
Eisley	0.878	0.778
Morris	0.480	0.648
Anderson	0.463	0.597
Carr	-0.015	0.560
Ostertag	0.188	0.565

Comments:

The Bulls were not at their best. Jordan and Pippen about 80% and 60% of their regular season performances. Scott Burrell played well, almost as well as Jordan.

Despite a 70% from Carl Malone the Jazz won from a magnificent 1.137 from Stockton and a supporting 0.878 from Eisley which even exceeded Jordan's 0.830 for that game.

Chicago 96, Utah 54

Utah:

Russell	0.310
Malone	0.690
Ostertag	0.208
Stockton	0.546
Hornacek	0.533
Eisley	0.320
Foster	0.059
Anderson	0.381
Morris	0.242
Carr	0.017
Keefe	0.467
Vaughn	0.029

Bulls:

Pippen	0.549
Kukoc	0.753
Longley	0.616
Harper	0.820
Jordan	0.888
Rodman	0.139
Burrell	0.576
Kerr	0.867
Buechler	0.867
Brown	0.560
Simpkins	0.880
Wennington	0.960

Comments:

In this match Chicago held Utah to a record low NBA score. The Utah Jazz was just awful in this game. All their players had a poor game on a day when most of the Bulls bench were above their EF averages, and gave very good performances. Jordan, Pippen, Kukoc, Rodman, and Longley were not the main contributors. Wennington's 0.960 was just outstanding.

NBA Finals 1997-98   -Bulls 87, Utah 86

Bulls:

Pippen	0.646
Kukoc	0.576
Longley	0.086
Jordan	1.100
Harper	0.517
Rodman	0.303
Burrell	0.000
Wennington	0.200
Kerr	0.242
Buechler	0.600

Utah:

Russell	0.324
Malone	1.088
Keefe	0.200
Hornacek	0.486
Stockton	0.588
Carr	0.392
Eisley	0.653
Morris	0.300
Anderson	0.463
Foster	-0.267

Comments:
Jordan was at his best during this final game with an EF of 1.100 but was matched by Malone's 1.088. Stockton was kept below his average and the performances by the Bulls was just enough to give them a win.

This match could have gone to the Jazz but fate was on Jordan's side. He won with the final basket of the game as the shot- clock ran down.

General
The EFs show exactly how the overall effort to a game, series, or even an era of success should be apportioned among the players. This method of analysis allows even more detailed performance monitoring of each player but such details are beyond the scope of this book. Teams should now be able to objectively analyze games and take the appropriate actions to ensure future success.

Part IV

Evaluating

The

Women

CHAPTER ELEVEN

The WNBA

The author is privileged to be writing this book just after the first season for the WNBA was completed. The WNBA began their competition in 1997 and all the team and individual statistics are now easily obtainable from the Internet.

Typical EFs for the WNBA will now be given. The following results were obtained on a team-by-team basis.

Charlotte Sting

Player	EF
Bullett	0.744
Stinson	0.741
Mapp	0.714
Hopson-Shelton	0.662
Suber	0.506
Congreaves	0.486
Manning	0.468
Moore	0.412
Levesque	0.401
Artis	0.315
Vukadinovic	0.286

Cleveland Rockers

Player	EF
Fijalkowski	0.659
Edwards	0.615
Braxton	0.607
Maxwell	0.600
Nemcova	0.579
Brown	0.559

Woodard	0.554
Jones	0.500
Nicholson	0.459
Johnson	0.348
Boucek	0.261

Houston Comets

Player	EF
Cooper	0.914
Swoops	0.716
Thompson	0.604
Arcain	0.541
Perrot	0.520
Harris	0.466
Jackson	0.356
Guyton	0.346
Woosley	0.344
Moore	0.209

New York Liberty

Player	EF
Hampton	0.658
Witherspoon	0.641
Wicks	0.635
Lobo	0.633
Weatherspoon	0.615
Johnson	0.519
Trice	0.479
Blades	0.457
Ford	0.388
Crumpton-Moorer	0.382

Los Angeles Sparks

Player	EF
Leslie	0.851
Toler	0.714
Haixia	0.645
Dixon	0.639
Mabika	0.605
Burge	0.562
Burgess	0.515
Wideman	0.464
Charles	0.435
Colleton	0.426
Gessig	-0.050

Phoenix Mercury

Player	EF
Timms	0.648
Pettis	0.648
Gillom	0.632
Askamp	0.608
Foster	0.544
Williams	0.536
Lieberman-Cline	0.514
Jackson	0.472
Webb	0.431
Ambers	0.351
Hagiwara	0.337

Sacramento Monarchs

Player	EF
Bolton-Holifield	0.747
Byears	0.623
Gordon	0.570
McGee	0.533
Tremitiere	0.455

Abraham	0.413
Yasen	0.391
Viglione	0.367
Savasta	0.321
Graves	0.312

Utah Starzz

Player	EF
Branova	0.703
Palmer	0.659
Williams	0.614
Head	0.544
Hicks	0.522
Reiss	0.478
Booker	0.471
Hardmon	0.414
Carter	0.385
Koss	0.297

The first championship match was won by the Houston Comets who defeated the New York Liberty 65-51, led by the 25 points from the first MVP, Cynthia Cooper.

The First WNBA Championship Match(1997)

The best EFs for that match were as follows:

Thompson	1.256	Comets
Cynthia Cooper	0.920	Comets
Hampton	0.580	New York
Johnson	0.524	New York
Lobo	0.412	New York

The statistics revealed that, as usual, the MVP, Cooper, had a great performance with an EF of 0.92. However, for that game the truly outstanding performance came from Thompson whose 1.256 EF was better than even Michael Jordan's in some games.

The performances from the New Yorkers was usually above 0.600. However, in that game they were all held to below their average performances. No one on New York's team should be blamed for this loss. It was a brilliant display by the Comets and the statistics suggest that on that night that team would have given even the 1997-98 NBA champions, the Bulls, a very competitive challenge.   If the Comets continue to play with such intensity, they will certainly be the first WNBA dynasty.

Some 1998 Performances:

Leslie	1.047
Cynthia Cooper	0.977
Swoopes	0.740
Lobo	0.684

Leslie gave the best overall effort for the season but Cynthia Cooper took home the championship again.

The Second WNBA Championship Match(1998)

Houston Comets 80, Phoenix Mercury 71:

Mercury:

Griffiths	0.880	B8
Pettis	0.710	B7
Gillom	0.678	B6
Timms	0.630	B6
Webb	0.600	B6

Average: B6

Comets:

Cooper	0.965	B9
Swoopes	0.941	B9
Perrot	0.688	B6
Thompson	0.616	B6
Lamb	0.507	B5

Average: B7

In this final players from both teams performed creditably.
Cynthia Cooper was in top form. Swoopes also performed very well.
Together they were just too much for Griffiths-Pettis duo.

On average, the Comets starters performed one grade level above the
Mercury's starters.

Part V

More

Tips

And

Tricks

CHAPTER TWELVE

Establishing and Maintaining Performance Standards

Basketball was invented in 1891 and already we are experiencing difficulty in maintaining proper performance records. Consider the confusion that will abound after another century passes. To avoid such a state, the governing bodies such as the NBA, the WNBA, the NCAA, and the ABA need to establish and maintain performance indices. Whenever a player retires, his or her performance index should be calculated from the career statistics and recorded for easy reference for future generations. If this is not done it will be very difficult to compare the great feats of players of today, such as Michael Jordan and Shaquille Oneal, with players ,say, two centuries in the future.

Before I began this study I shared the same opinion with most others that an objective comparison of basketballers of different eras was impossible. However, I later found out after some brainstorming that the hypothesis was wrong. Basketballers of all eras had something in common that equally opposed them over the years-TIME. I realized that if players were allowed to play one-on-one with TIME they could be essentially compared with each other. If the amount of "work" each player averaged per minute was quantified then they could be compared by the value each obtained- the EF.

All the tasks performed during a game were identified. Only turnovers were negative contributors. All the other elements such as points-scored, rebounds, steals, and assists, are positive work. To sum a player's work for each session, all the elements had to be converted to a common base. The most appropriate unit seemed to be points but anyone of the work elements could have been used as the common unit. So, all the elements were converted to points, summed, and divided by the total time the player took to accomplish those statistics. This algorithm solved the problem. The rate at which players build their statistics less the rate a which they turned- over the ball compared players of different eras accurately. The results obtained were consistent with the written reports about the players throughout history and further confirmed by personal observations and current player statistics.

One of the primary activity of engineers even while on campus is the development, approval, and application of standards for all their operations. Electrical engineers are expected to prepare their designs in accordance with national standards such as ANSI (American National Standards Institute) or NEMA(National Manufacturers Electrical Association. In my first few years with a power company I had to constantly use their design standards. There were standards for:

- .selecting and installing cables
- grounding equipment
- lighting substations
- erecting and grouting structures
installing conduits

There were scores of standards to learn. I later discovered that the true "greatness" of an engineer was in his or her ability to apply the applicable standard appropriately. One major event somewhat changed my life. Once, my department submitted a contract document, to the construction department, which was returned to us for the inclusion of a section on conduit installation. The constructors needed to know the size conduit to be run from the cable trenches to the panels of the equipment.

I was a young engineer but the most senior in my department, as the more experienced engineers had been temporarily transferred to assist with construction projects. I was surprised when my boss asked me to develop the standard for inclusion in such an important document. Afterwards, I began to understand that such activities were normal for an engineer. So, it is very difficult for me to simply accept that basketballers of different eras could not- I needed to find a solution. I learned early to never tell my boss "I can't" but rather "I'll try". If you consistently fail to do your job, the company will find someone who can ,even if it has to employ consultants. Given this task on the job , I would have been expected to solve it.

My exposure to units and standards began in college. I lived on campus with a group of students who delighted in identifying and applying standards. Typical examples of our "arbitrary" standards are given:

- Anyone Bright - unit of study
- Noname Calling-unit of womanizing
- Sloppy Person-unit of sleep

Engineering studies trained me to conceptualize and complete projects. Now I can see clearly how basketballers across the decades may be compared. Most of us are familiar with music equalizers and their ability to show the frequency components of music with panel LEDs (light emitting diodes).

Consider the frequency bandwidths to be replaced by the elements of a basketballer's statistics. We would now be able to graphically observe the fluctuations of each element. This, however, would not allow us to make live-game decisions fast enough. To remedy this situation, an indicator for the total effort would be needed. This would receive inputs from all the other indicators, summed by electronic circuitry. The Total- indicator, if interpreted literally, could give misleading results. Players totals will depend on the number of seasons they played. A mediocre player for 12 years could easily have a greater total than one who performed excellently for, say, eight years. To further rationalize the system, the rate at which the Total is attained must be monitored-EF. Basketballers across different eras can be compared fairly from their EFs.

Another very important concept to add to your knowledge base will now be considered. Let us make Michael Jordan the unit of basketball performance. So, an EF of 1.357 -Michael Jordan(1988-89)- will be given the value of one jordan. That is :

1.357=1 jordan

Using this equation the top players of all times are :

Rank	Player	EF	jordans
01	Joe Fulks	1.958	1.4
02	George Mikan(career)	1.792	1.3
03	Max Zaslofsky	1.556	1.2
04	Magic Johnson(86-87)	1.443	1.1
05	Michael Jordan(88-89)	1.357	1.0
06	John Stockton(89-90)	1.308	0.96
07	Shaquille Oneal(97-98)	1.270	0.94
08	David Robinson(93-94)	1.257	0.93
09	Gail Goodrich(71-72)	1.219	0.89
10	Jerry West(71-72)	1.214	0.89
	Olajuwon(92-93)	1.201	0.88
	Patrick Ewing(89-90)	1.186	0.87
	Kareem. Abdul Jabbar(79-80)	1.184	0.87
	Bob Cousy(59-60)	1.169	0.86
	Tim Hardaway(90-91)	1.154	0.85
	Karl Malone(96-97)	1.136	0.84

The above exercise give results that may be interpreted in a variety of ways. For example it suggests that Fulk at his best was 40% more efficient than

Jordan at his best. Also, that the best Jordan was 16% more effective than Karl Malone. Other players may be more easily compared too. It suggests that Tim Hardaway 's effort level is generally very similar to Bob Cousy's.

One of the most important principle learned from all this talk on standards is that we all need to establish and maintain standards of personal behavior regardless of our lot in life. Some of the best standards all basketballers and other athletes should hold dear include good sportsmanship and an excellent team spirit.

A Basketball Board Game

Another useful way to explain the concept of EF is to view basketball as a board-game similar to Scrabble or Boggle. The rules of this new game will not be considered now, only the system of scoring.

This would be a two-player game. Each player would alternately roll five dice each of which had basketball tasks and corresponding scores recorded as follows:

- side 1- Points-scored   10
- side 2-Assists-   5
- side-3 Rebounds   2
- side 4-Steals   3
- side-5 Blocks   4
- side 6-Turn-overs   0

After 25 tosses of the group of five dice, the totals for each player could be obtained and the player with the higher total declared the winner. In this case, considering the time for each player would not be necessary as each player was given the same number of tosses. However, we could use a similar system for live games. Players could be given scores for each task they accomplished. At the end of a game, each player's total score would be calculated. However, as each player normally plays for different durations, it would be unfair to simply compare the totals. A comparison of the rates at which each one achieved his or her total would be the value to use for fair comparisons. This rate of building one's statistics is what EF measures.

Let us consider another example in which each player-file is analogous to a basket to which an appropriate number of marbles are added for every point, assist, steal, rebound, and blocks, the player makes. Two marbles are removed each time a turn-over is committed. The player, whose amassed, say, 2000 marbles first is the greatest, regardless of the era in which that feat was accomplished.

Standard Team

Having studied the best teams, I averaged the top six EFs from each team and ranked them accordingly. The Philadelphia 76ers of 1966-67 was adjudged to be the best team on this basis. The average EF for that team was 0.942 while Wilt Chamberlain's EF was 1.086. So, Chamberlain contributed to about $\{(1.086)/(0.948 \times 6) \times 100\}\%$ or 19% of his team's effort. From the above discussion we may develop another formula:

0.942= 1 sixers

The ranking order of the teams using formula is:

Rank	Team	sixers
01	1966-67 Philadelphia 76ers	1.000
02	1986-87 Los Angeles Lakers	0.990
03	1982-83 Philadelphia 76ers	0.989
04	1959-60 Boston Celtics	0.979
05	1985-86 Boston Celtics	0.974
06	1971-72 Los Angeles Lakers	0.969
07	1986-87 Los Angeles Lakers	0.966
08	1979-80 Los Angeles Lakers	0.944
09	1970-71 Milwaukee Bucks	0.943
10	188-89 Detroit Pistons	0.913
11	1964-65 Boston Celtics	0.898
12	1990-91 Chicago Bulls	0.878
13	1969-70 New York Knicks	0.818
14	1993-94 Houston Rockets	0.868
15	1995-96 Chicago Bulls	0.831
16**	1949-50 Minnesota Lakers	0.588

The top five teams would be very difficult to rank by subjective methods as they all performed with about the same effectiveness and it would have been very difficult for the human observer to discern the difference.

NBA Finals 1997-98 Season- Chicago 87, Utah Jazz 86

This game was chiefly a contest between Michael Jordan and Karl Malone as the other players effectively nullified each other. The team EFs for this game were:

Chicago= 0.624
Utah   = 0.612

On that night the teams effectively prevented each other from making big scores. They both performed way below their regular season bests, at levels that could have been seemingly competitively contested by any team in the league. This was a highly defensive game.

Stockton and Malone missed a great opportunity to get their first ring. This brings to mind Max Zaslofsky who was repeatedly beaten by Mikan - one great player defeating another great player. Stockton and Malone are great players who along with Patrick Ewing, Shaquille Oneal, David Robinson, Charles Barkley and many others, have been repeatedly denied by Michael Jordan.

By writing this book I am not suggesting that my EF formula should be the world standard. I am only showing how the development of one is possible and some of the benefits to be derived if basketballers developed such a system. To arrive at a world standard, the WNBA, NBA, Olympic Committee, and other major sporting authorities would need to form a new standards group. This group would be responsible for establishing and maintaining the standards and to develop new measuring units.

One other activity the standards group could undertake is the grading and ranking of every basketballer to play professionally, worldwide. Players would be graded and ranked at the end of each season. Every rookie should also be officially graded before entering the professional leagues. Each player could be charged a small fee for an official certificate. This should generate enough revenue to keep the standards committee operational.

CHAPTER THIRTEEN

Making Strategic Decisions

It appears that no team will suffer if it only replaces players with ones having greater EFs. This may not always be possible because of salary caps and the unavailability of the needed players. Also, the statistics cannot detail the character, attitude, and team-spirit of players. So, the EF comparison should only be used as a general starting guide and the final decisions based on the judgment of experienced recruiters.

A. Player Substitution Rules

As EF is a function of time, the mathematical operation of differentiation can be performed on it (high-school math). With a little research those of us who did not sleep during math classes will recall that:

$$\frac{d(x^n)}{dx} = nx^{n-1}$$

Given that:

$$Z = (2Ast + PTS + 0.4R + 0.4 STLS + 2BLK - 0.6TO)$$

$$\therefore \ EF = Z/TMP$$

i.e. $EF = (Z)TMP^{-1}$

so, $\frac{d(EF)}{dt} = -Z \times TMP^{-2}$

It would be wise to rest a player as soon as the rate of change of EF becomes negative. As TMP is always positive, for this to be achieved Z must be equal to zero:

i.e. $Z = 0$

total positive contribution = total negative contribution

In this case,

$$0.6TO = 2AST + PTS + 0.4R + 0.4 STLS + 2BLK$$

As long as $0.6TO < (2AST + PTS + 0.4R + 0.4 STLS + 2BLK)$

a player is making a positive contribution to his or her team.
This approximates to:

$$TO < (3AST + 2PTS + R + STLS + 3BLKS)$$

Considering that players have attacking and defensive roles a series of equations may be deduced to quickly determine if a player should be rested:

1. **TO<3AST**

2. **TO<2PTS**

3. **TO<R**

4. **TO<STLS**

5. **TO<3BLKS**

At any instant in a game a player's stats should satisfy the above equations or any combination of them or that player's overall contribution is negative. How long a coach continues with a player in such situations depends on the particular circumstance, however.

CHAPTER FOURTEEN
Coaching Tips

The EF formula, as given, is too complicated to be used by coaches during live games. Also, an electronic calculator is not allowed on the bench. To control a game, coaches need to monitor it properly and have decision- making, feedback information readily available. One way this could be done is by using a modified EF formula for game situations.

Assigning all the work elements a value of one unit gives:

EF(modified)= (AST+PTS+R+STL + BLK -TO)/TMP

If a player's EF is calculated at three minute intervals, say, the variations in his or her performance can be easily monitored. To compare performances the same formula should be used for each game. It should be noted that a players EF cannot be properly monitored if that player is not given enough play-time(TMP). The development of an EF Tables, similar to sine, cosine, and other mathematics tables, could be a solution.

Part VI

Player

Appraisals

CHAPTER FIFTEEN

Evaluating Players

Using EF allows us to monitor players over any time-frame. Below, the EF performance analyses of a few players are given.

Player	Year	EF

Penny Hardaway:

	Year	EF
	1993-94	0.914
	1994-95	1.018
	1995-96	1.073
	1996-97	0.939
	1997-98	0.830

Penny was at his best in 1996. In 1998 he gave an average output which was less than his effort five years earlier. He is still a good player but is way below his top form.

Charles Barkley:

	Year	EF
	1985-86	1.002
	1986-87	1.051
	1987-88	1.072
	1988-89	1.058
	1989-90	1.013
	1990-91	1.120
	1991-92	0.979
	1992-93	1.148
	1993-94	1.044
	1994-95	1.070
	1995-96	1.010
	1996-97	0.934
	1997-98	0.795

Charles is a grade A player who has performed consistently over the years. He peaked in 1993 and his better days seem to be behind him.

Sam Cassell:

1993-94	0.816
1994-95	0.926
1995-96	0.919
1996-97	1.003
1997-98	1.034

Sam has been steadily improving since 1993. He is now one of the better players in the NBA. His 1998 EF is even better than his 1993 effort.

Tim Hardaway:

1989-90	1.034
1990-91	1.154
1991-92	1.117
1992-93	1.147
1994-95	1.094
1995-96	1.056
1996-97	1.028
1997-98	0.971

Tim is a very good player. 1993 was his best year. Since then his performance has been steadily declining each year. He still "got game", however.

David Robinson:

1989-90	1.135
1990-91	1.174
1991-92	1.149
1992-93	1.084
1993-94	1.257
1994-95	1.184
1995-96	1.170
1996-97	1.067
1997-98	1.046

David's best EF was his 1994 value. His 1.257 showed that he is one of the best ever.

Scottie Pippen:

1987-88	0.741
1988-89	0.794
1989-90	0.872
1990-91	0.990
1991-92	1.063
1992-93	0.957
1993-94	1.031
1994-95	1.007
1995-96	0.979
1996-97	0.954
1997-98	0.904

Scottie's 1.063, in 1993, was his best. He is now on the decline but is still presently one of the best.

Shaquille Oneal :

1992-93	1.056
1993-94	1.144
1994-95	1.203
1995-96	1.144
1996-97	1.145
1997-98	1.128

Shaquille's best effort so far was his 1995 output. He is performing even better than when he began.

Alonzo Mourning:

1992-93	1.008
1993-94	1.036
1994-95	0.897
1995-96	0.988
1996-97	0.940
1997-98	0.831

Alone peaked in 1994. He is still a good player but is now not at his best.

Karl Malone:

1985-86	0.828
1986-87	0.895
1987-88	0.988
1988-89	1.038
1989-90	1.107
1990-91	1.050
1991-92	1.054
1992-93	1.088
1993-94	1.005
1994-95	1.048
1995-96	1.037
1996-97	1.136
1997-98	1.051

Karl is definitely a grade A0 player with flashes of A1 brilliance. He is now one of the NBA's best.

Michael Jordan:

1984-85	1.178
1985-86	1.322
1986-87	1.314
1987-88	1.324
1988-89	1.357
1989-90	1.319
1990-91	1.298
1991-92	1.228
1992-93	1.244
1994-95	1.081
1995-96	1.155
1996-97	1.118
1997-98	0.990

Michael Jordan "His Airness" is definitely one of the best players to ever play basketball. His EFs, over the years, has been matched by very few players. He is the best player of the 90's.

George Mikan:

1951-52	0.878
1952-53	0.848
1953-54	0.874
1955-56	0.809
Regular Season	1.714
Playoffs	1.504
All Star	1.124

Mikan started off as a B8 player in 1952 but had an extra-ordinary career, raising his game to level A7 for his career average., the second highest EF obtained so far.

Allen Iverson:

1996-97	1.037
1997-98	0.901

Allen has great talent. He needs to guard his effort so that he does not burnout and decline too quickly.

Grant Hill:

1994-95	0.915
1995-96	0.970
1996-97	1.054
1997-98	0.928

Grant, peaked in 1997. He is still a very good player. He has great potential.

Patrick Ewing:

1985-86	0.909
1986-87	0.959
1987-88	1.062
1988-89	1.069
1989-90	1.186
1990-91	1.144
1991-92	1.008
1992-93	1.001
1993-94	1.050
1994-95	1.028
1995-96	0.988
1996-97	0.971
1997-98	0.918

Patrick is also one of the best. For most of his career he has been a A0 player but for the last two years (97 and 98) he has declined to B9.

Rod Strickland:

1988-89	1.081
1989-90	0.928
1990-91	0.907
1991-92	0.953
1992-93	0.979
1993-94	1.089
1994-95	1.116
1995-96	1.079
1996-97	1.029
1997-98	1.011

Rod's usual efforts are in the A1-B9 ranges. Currently, he is A0, which is very good.

John Stockton:

1984-85	0.937
1985-86	1.036
1986-87	1.156
1987-88	1.296
1988-89	1.220
1989-90	1.308
1990-91	1.277
1991-92	1.265
1992-93	1.198
1993-94	1.187
1994-95	1.203
1995-96	1.104
1996-97	1.067
1997-98	1.011

Very few players attain grade A3 in any year of their career. John has been one of them. His efforts make him one of the top 10 players of all time.

Hakeem Olajuwon:

1984-85	0.955
1985-86	1.094
1986-87	1.124
1987-88	1.065
1988-89	1.132
1989-90	1.199
1990-91	1.090
1991-92	1.070

1992-93	1.201
1993-94	1.155
1994-95	1.178
1995-96	1.152
1996-97	1.038
1997-98	0.852

Hakeem is now on the decline but his performance over the years places him as one of the top players of all-time.

EF analysis may be done for any duration, even in live games. As an example, the monthly variations in performance in 1997-98 were investigated and gave:

Tim Hardaway: 1997-98

Month	Games	EF
October	1	1.443
November	14	1.042
December	14	1.097
January	14	0.940
February	15	0.959
March	15	1.037
April	08	0.977

Tim's performance in October 1997 was similar to that usually given by Magic Johnson. His EF fluctuated from A4 in October to B9 in April 1998. It would have been wonderful if he could have finished the season with his best. He has great potential but needs to manage his output each game so that he can enter the play-offs at his peak.

Michael Jordan:1997-98

Month	Games	EF
October	01	1.029
November	15	1.003
December	14	1.052
January	16	1.042
February	13	0.974

| March | 14 | 1.006 |
| April | 9 | 1.090 |

Michael gave an A0 performance for most of the regular season. Going into the playoffs he was among the most effective players in the league. On the day of the NBA finals, he was at his peak(A1), and was the best. Jordan practices better energy management than most other players of his time. During the regular season he only averaged B9.

General Comments

Winning the NBA Championship is not an easy task. It involves great physical fitness and mental preparation. Contrary to what many believe, the road to the championship starts with the first regular season game. All players need to monitor and control their aggregate output ensuring that they have enough energy when it matters most-during the finals.

Part VII

Determining

The

Greatest

Team

Ever

CHAPTER SIXTEEN

Determining the Greatest Team Ever

1949-50 Minnesota   Lakers:

George Mikan	1.130
Jim Pollard	0.739
Vern Mikkelsen	0.519
P. Walther(Tot)	0.202
Arnie Ferrin	0.265
Herm Schaefer	0.368
Don Carlson	0.210
B. Hassett (Tot)	0.273
Bob Harrison	0.281
Slater Martin	0.284
Tony Jaros	0.180
G. Stump (Tot)	0.126
Bud Grant	0.065
Norman Glick	0.001

The total minutes played (TMP) for the players was not recorded so each was given an estimated value of 2000. So, the EFs for this team are estimated values. The top six players EF average was 0.554.

1959-60 Boston Celtics :

Tom Heinsohn	0.946
Bob Cousy	1.169
Bill Sharman	0.920
Bill Russell	0.831
Frank Ramsey	0.793
Sam Jones	0.845
Maury King	0.821
Gene Conley	0.585

K. C. Jones	0.725
Jim Loscutoff	0.413
John Richter	0.574
Gene Guarilia	0.508

Top six EF average=0.922

1964-65 Boston Celtics :

Sam Jones	0.929
John Havlicek	0.886
Bill Russell	0.771
Tom Heinsohn	0.812
Thomas Sanders	0.565
Willie Naulls	0.700
K. C. Jones	0.678
Ron Bonham	0.930
Larry Siegfried	0.750
Mel Counts	0.703
John Thompson	0.506
Robert Nordmann	0.608
Gerry Ward	0.633

Top six EF average =   0.846

1966-67 Philadelphia 76ers :

Wilt Chamberlain	1.086
Hal Greer	0.823
Chet Walker	0.820
Billy Cunningham	0.987
Wali Jones	0.792
Lucious Jackson	0.626
Larry Costello	0.718
Dave Gambee	0.753
Bill Melchionni	0.795
Matt Guokas	0.557
Bob Weiss	1.145

Top six EF average = 0.942

1969-70 New York Knicks :

Willis Reed	0.818
Walt Frazier	1.004
Dick Barnett	0.687
Dave Debusschere	0.707
Bill Bradley	0.764
Cazzie Russell	0.805
Dave Stallworth	0.761
Mike Riordan	0.658
Wilmer Hosket	0.754
Nate Bowman	0.580
Don May	0.634
Johnny Warren	0.691

Top six EF average = 0.818

1970-71 Milwaukee Bucks :

K. Abdul-Jabbar	1.114
Oscar Robertson	0.967
Bob Dandridge	0.789
Jon McGlocklin	0.689
Greg Smith	0.679
Bob Boozer	0.652
Lucius Allen	0.702
M. McLemore	0.643
M. McLemore	0.564
G. Freeman	0.756
Marv Winkler	0.971
D. Cunningham	0.577
Bob Greacen	0.777
Jeff Webb	0.375
Bill Zopf	0.710

Top six EF average = 0.888

1971-72 LA Lakers :

Gail Goodrich	0.979
Jerry West	1.214
Jim McMillian	0.698
Wilt Chamberlain	0.721
Happy Hairston	0.674
Elgin Baylor	0.690
Flynn Robinson	0.950
Pat Riley	0.702
Keith Erickson	0.655
John Trapp	0.639
Leroy Ellis	0.516
Jim Cleamons	0.913

Top six EF average=0.913

1979-80 LA Lakers :

Kareem Abdul-Jabbar	1.184
Jamaal Wilkes	0.791
Magic Johnson	1.041
Norm Nixon	0.902
Jim Chones	0.647
S. Haywood	0.770
Michael Cooper	0.692
M. Landsberger	0.668
M. Landsberger	0.717
R. Boone	0.513
K. Carr (LAL)	0.484
D. Ford (LAL)	0.518
Brad Holland	0.837
Marty Byrnes	0.535
O. Mack (LAL)	0.654
B. Lee (Tot)	0.851

Top six EF average = 0.889

1982-83 Philadelphia 76ers :

Moses Malone	1.005
Julius Erving	1.062
Andrew Toney	1.004
Maurice Cheeks	0.931
Bobby Jones	0.745

Clint Richardson	0.620
C. Johnson (Tot)	0.735
C. Johnson (Phi)	0.588
Franklin Edwards	0.839
R. Johnson (Tot)	0.613
R. Johnson (Phi)	0.509
Marc Iavaroni	0.498
R. Schoene (Phi)	0.544
Earl Cureton	0.512
Mark McNamara	0.712
M. Anderson	0.504

Top six EF average = 0.931

1985-86 Boston Celtics :

Larry Bird	1.195
Kevin McHale	0.964
Robert Parish	0.842
Dennis Johnson	0.859
Danny Ainge	0.752
Scott Wedman	0.668
Bill Walton	0.893
Jerry Sichting	0.611
David Thirdkill	0.601
Sam Vincent	0.824
Sly Williams	0.544
Rick Carlisle	0.597
Greg Kite	0.486

Top six EF average = 0.918

1986-87 LA Lakers :

Magic Johnson	1.443
James Worthy	0.866
K. Abdul-Jabbar	0.899
Byron Scott	0.791
A. C. Green	0.649
Michael Cooper	0.809
M. Thompson (Tot)	0.790
M. Thompson (LAL)	0.749
Kurt Rambis	0.571

Billy Thompson	0.770
Adrian Branch	0.930
Wes Matthews	0.835
F. Brickowski (LAL)	0.550
Mike Smrek	0.551

Top six EF average = 0.933

1995-96 Chicago Bulls:

Michael Jordan	1.154
Toni Kukoc	0.876
Scottie Pippen	0.767
Luc Longley	0.671
Ron Harper	0.637
Steve Kerr	0.591
Bill Wennington	0.539
Dennis Rodman	0.537

Top six EF average = 0.783

1993-94 Houston Rockets :

H. Oulajuwon	1.155
Sam Cassell	0.816
Vernon Maxwell	0.764
Kenny Smith	0.745
Mario Ellie	0.716
Robert Horry	0.691
Otis Thorpe	0.673
Chris Jent	0.654

Top six EF average = 0.815

1990-91 Chicago Bulls:

Michael Jordan	1.319
Scottie Pippen	0.872
Horace Grant	0.720
B.J. Armstrong	0.714
John Paxson	0.669
Stacey King	0.668
Bill Cartwright	0.634
Craig Hodges	0.630
Will Perdue	0.601

Top-six EF average = 0.827

188-89 Detroit Pistons :

Isiah Thomas	1.021
M. Aguirre	0.890
Joe Dumars	0.860
Vinnie Johnson	0.858
A. Dantley	0.779
Bill Laimbeer	0.754
Dennis Rodman	0.641

Top six EF average = 0.860

The ranking order of the teams are:

01	1966-67 Philadelphia 76ers	0.942
02	1986-87 Los Angeles Lakers	0.933
03	1982-83 Philadelphia 76ers	0.931
04	1959-60 Boston Celtics	0.922
05	1985-86 Boston Celtics	1.918
06	1971-72 Los Angeles Lakers	0.913
07	1986-87 Los Angeles Lakers	0.910
08	1979-80 Los Angeles Lakers	0.889
09	1970-71 Milwaukee Bucks	0.888
10	188-89 Detroit Pistons	0.860
. 11	1964-65 Boston Celtics	0.846
12	1990-91 Chicago Bulls	0.827
13	1969-70 New York knicks	0.818
14	1993-94 Houston Rockets	0.815
15	1995-96 Chicago Bulls	0.783
16**	1949-50 Minnesota Lakers	0.554

** Estimated time played was used. It is suspected that this was over-estimated, thus the low rating of this team. These results suggest that the players of the previous decades were much more effective than our modern players and that the 1966-67 76ers were the best team ever. This team was able to accomplish more per minute of play than all the other teams.

The Boston Celtics:

Throughout history this team has been blessed with great players. Many of the early championships were largely attributed to Bill Russell but it was rather a team effort from a great group of players. Some of the best EFs achieved by Boston players over the decades were:

Larry Bird (85-86)	1.195
Kevin McHale(85-86)	0.964)
Bill Walton(85-86)	0.893
Dennis Johnson(85-86)	0.859
Danny Ainge	0.752
Robert Parish(80-81)	1.136
Larry Bird (80-81)	0.985
Sam Jones(64-65)	0.929
Bob Cousy(59-60)	1.169
Tom Heinsohn(59-60)	0.946
Bill Russell(59-60)	0.831
Bill Sharman(59-60)	0.828

Part VIII

Epilogue

Conclusions

This study has confirmed that Michael Jordan is the best player of the 90's and has revealed that the Joe Fulks gave the greatest ever performance to win the first championship. Mikan then dominated and was in fact voted by the *Associated Press* as the best player for the first half-century. His career EF was so high that originally it seemed as if a data entry error had been made.

These methods confirmed that Cynthia Cooper is currently the best of the women and that our present all-stars would have been stars in any era. With practice, whenever a player's EF is mentioned it will cause one to immediately associate it with a that of a familiar player. For example, when Alonzo Mourning scored 30 points against the Knicks , in the 1997-98 playoffs , on a day when he made almost all his shots, his EF was the same as that of Olajuwon when he led the Houston Rockets to NBA championships in the early '90s.

The title of *Best Team Ever* went to the 1966-67 Philadelphia 76ers led by Wilt Chamberlain.

Glossary

Air ball: A missed shot that does not touch the rim or backboard.

Alley-hoop shot: A shot made by a player who while running towards the basket, leaps high and catches the ball, thrown by a second player, in midair, and dunks it or lays it in before he lands.

Assist: A pass to a teammate that leads directly to a basket.

Backcourt: A team's defensive half of the court. As it refers to players, a team's guards.

Backdoor play: A fundamental basketball play in which one player passes to a teammate in the high post, and when the defenders follow the ball, another player cuts to the basket from the opposite side of the court to take a pass for an open shot.

Bank shot: A shot that is aimed at a spot on the backboard so that it bounces, or "banks," into the basket.

Baseline: The line at each end of the court, under each basket. Also: endline. Bench: Reserves.

Blind Pass: A pass made by a player to a teammate without looking at that teammate.

Bounce pass: A pass thrown by a player to a teammate that bounces on the floor.

Box out: Use your body to stay between an opponent and the basket and thus get into better position for a rebound.

Brick: A hard, errant shot that caroms wildly off the basket or backboard.

Bunny: An open, uncontested shot, usually a lay-up or dunk. Also: snowbird.

Bury: Sink (a shot), as in "bury a jumper."

Charging: A violation in which an offensive player runs into a stationary opponent.

Chucker: A player who never met a shot he didn't like.

Coast-to-coast: From one end of the court to the other.

Collective Bargaining Agreement: The agreement between the NBA and the Players Association that governs all terms and conditions of employment of NBA players by NBA teams.

Cut: A quick move by an offensive player, usually toward the basket, to get in position for a shot.

Dead-ball foul: A foul committed while the clock is stopped and the ball is not in play. Deny the ball: Prevent an opponent from getting the ball by guarding him closely and staying between him and the player in possession of the ball.

Double dribble: A violation in which a player dribbles the ball, stops, then begins to dribble again.

Double-team: The defensive tactic of two players guarding one.

Downtown: Far from the basket, often synonymous with beyond the three-point arc.

Draft: The annual selection process by which NBA teams select players from the colleges and elsewhere.

Dribble: Bounce the ball.

Dunk: A shot thrown downward through the basket, with one or two hands. Also: slam, slam-dunk, jam

Fast break: A play in which a team gains possession and then pushes the ball downcourt quickly, hoping to get a good shot off before the other team has a chance to get back and set up on defense.

Field goal: A basket, worth either two or three points, depending on whether it was taken from inside or outside the three-point line (set at 22 feet from the basket).

Flagrant foul: Unnecessary and/or excessive contact committed against an opponent.

Foul: A violation. Usually, illegal contact between two players.

Foul trouble: When a player is nearing the limit for personal fouls before he is ejected from the game, or a team is nearing the limit in each period after which all fouls become shooting fouls.

Free agent: A player not under contract to any NBA team because his contract has expired or was terminated by his team in accordance with NBA waiver procedures, or because he was eligible for an NBA Draft and was never signed to an NBA contract.

Free throw: An uncontested shot from 15 feet, worth one point. A player who is fouled while in the act of shooting receives two free throws. Also: foul shot.

Frontcourt: A team's offensive half of the court. As it refers to players, a team's center and forwards.

Give-and-go: A fundamental play in which one player passes to a teammate, then cuts to the basket to receive a return pass for an open lay-up or dunk.

Goaltending: A violation in which a player interferes with a shot while the ball is on its downward arc, pins it against the backboard or touches it while it is in an imaginary cylinder above the basket; may be committed by either an offensive or defensive player.

Gunner: A frequent shooter.

Hand-checking: A violation in which a defender uses his hand to impede a player's progress.

Hang time: The amount of time a player can stay in the air while attempting a shot.

High post: The area around the free throw circle.

Hook shot: A shot taken with a sweeping, hooking motion. May be taken stationary or while running.

Hoop: Basket or rim. Also slang for playing basketball. :

Jump ball: When players from opposing teams gain simultaneous possession of the ball, the referee stops play. After the teams are realigned, he tosses the ball up between two players, who attempt to tap it to a teammate.

Jump hook: A hook shot taken while jumping, popular among big men because it is difficult to block.

Jump shot: A shot taken after a player jumps in the air.

Key: The free throw lane and circle.

Lane: The painted area between the end line and the free-throw line near each basket, outside which players line up for free throws. Also known as the key, because in the early years it was key-shaped. It was twice widened to its present rectangular shape.

Loose-ball foul: A foul committed while neither team has possession of the ball, as while going for a rebound.

Lottery: The process that determines the order of selection, among the non-playoff teams, in the first round of the draft.

Low post: The area at the base of the foul lane to either side of the basket.

Net: The cord, 15 to 18 inches long, that hangs from the rim of the basket.

Outlet pass: A pass thrown by a player after getting a rebound to a teammate, generally near midcourt, to start a fast break.

Over the limit: Beyond a given number of fouls. Each team is allowed four fouls per quarter for which no free throws are assessed (unless they are committed against players in the act of shooting); after four fouls a team is said to be "over the limit" and free throws are assessed on all subsequent fouls.

Overtime: A five-minute extra period that is played when the game is tied after four quarters. If a game remains tied following an overtime period, another is played and another until there is a winner.

Palming: A violation in which a player moves his hand under the ball and scoops it while dribbling. Also: carrying the ball.

Penalty situation: When a team has committed more than its allotted four fouls per quarter and thus each subsequent foul becomes a shooting foul. Also: Over the limit.

Personal foul: see Foul.

Pick: When an offensive player frees a teammate for a shot by establishing a stationary position that prevents a defensive player from guarding the shooter. If the player who is "setting a pick" is not stationary and contact is made with a defender, it is an offensive foul and his team loses possession of the ball. Also: screen.

Pick-and-roll: A play in which an offensive player sets a pick, then "rolls" toward the basket and takes a pass from a teammate for an open shot.

Pill: Ball.

Pivot: The area near the basket, generally where the center operates, or the act of changing directions, by keeping one foot planted on the ground while stepping in one or more directions with the other foot.

Post: see Low Post.

Player-control foul: An offensive foul that is committed not when a player is shooting, but just when his team is in control of the ball.

Point guard: Usually a team's primary ballhandler and the man who sets up the team's offense.

Power forward: The larger of a team's two forwards, whose duties generally involve rebounding as much as scoring.

Press: Guard very closely.

Pump fake: A fake in which a player motions as if he is going to shoot the ball but holds back, hoping his defender will jump out of position.

Quadruple-double: An extremely rare (it's only happened four times in NBA history) achievement in which a player accumulates doubles figures in four of the following categories in the same game: points, rebounds, assists, steals and blocked shots.

Rebound: Gather in and gain control of a missed shot; a missed shot that is retrieved.

Rejection: A blocked shot. Rock: Ball.

Sag: A defensive tactic in which a player drops off his man to help double-team a player in the pivot.

Salary Cap: Common term for Maximum Team Salary, the maximum amount each team may pay in salaries during an NBA season, as per teams of the Collective Bargaining Agreement.

Screen: Pick. Set shot: A shot taken while a player has both feet on the floor in a set position. Common in basketball's early years, it is now all but extinct, having given way to the harder-to-block jump shot.

Shot clock: The 24-second clock used to time possessions. A team must attempt a shot that hits the rim within 24 seconds or else it loses possession of the ball.

Sixth man: A team's primary reserve, the first substitute to enter a game.

Sky-hook: A hook shot in which the ball is released while the shooter's hand is at the top of the arc; used most effectively by Kareem Abdul-Jabbar, the NBA's all-time career scoring leader.

Skywalk: The ability to move laterally while in the air.

Slam dunk: see Dunk.

Steal: To take the ball away from the opposing team, either off the dribble or by picking off a pass.

Stuff: To forcibly block an attempted shot or to ram the ball into the hoop.

Switch: When teammates exchange defensive assignments during play.

Technical foul: The penalty for a violation of conduct, such as abusive language or fighting. Each technical foul awards a free throw to the opposing team and also means an automatic fine for the player who commits the violation.

Three-point shot: A field goal worth three points, taken from beyond an arc that is 22 feet from the basket.

Three-second violation: An offensive player may not stand in the lane for three seconds.

360: To elude a defender by doing a complete spin, making a 360-degree turn.

Tip-in: To tip a missed shot into the basket.

Trailer: An offensive player who trails on a fast break but often is in good position to score after the first wave of defenders goes by.

Transition: The movement from offense to defense, or vice versa, when the ball changes hands.

Traveling: A violation in which a player takes too many steps without dribbling the ball. Also: walking.

Triple-double: A relatively rare achievement in which a player accumulates double figures in three of the following categories in the same game: points, rebounds, assists, steals and blocked shots.

Turnover: Loss of ball, either through an errant pass or dribble or an offensive foul.

Veteran free agent: A player who completes his contractual obligation to his team and becomes free to sign with any NBA team, as per terms of the Collective Bargaining Agreement.

Weak side: The side of the court away from the ball.

Zone: A defensive tactic in which players guard areas of the court, rather than specific men.

References

The Official NBA Encyclopedia by The NBA Staff

The World Almanac and Book of Facts by Funk and Wagnalls Corp

ATHLON® SPORTS™PRO BASKETBALL EDITION VOL 5 / 1998-99

Basketball Biographies byMartinTaragano

Websites

http://www.nba.com
http://www.cbs.sportsline.com/u/basketball/nba/players
http://www.geocities.com/colosseum/pressbox/5326
http://espn.sportszone.com
http://www.wnba.com
http://www.polydor.com/mercury/artists/nba/early_years.html
http://www.newsday.com/sports/hoops/knxgm1.htm
http://www.cleveland.com/sports/allstar/evolution/small.html
http://www.kentuckyconnect.com/heraldleader/news/1030/fs30list.html
http://www.members.aol.com/apbrhoops/labor.html

A Word Of Caution

The formula for EF is a very good mathematical model of a basketballer's performance. The author guarantees that if this formula is applied to all your data, the values obtained will facilitate very accurate player comparisons. The author makes no guarantee, however, as to the usefulness or accuracy of the data given in this book for the reader's particular purpose. Users are encouraged to confirm their own calculations before using EFs to make any major decision. Slight variations of the constants in the formula should
 not affect the results significantly as all the players would still be subjected to the same formula. Changes should be carefully considered, however.

Using the copy-paste and the automatic calculation features of a spreadsheet reduces calculation efforts.

The concept of EF is sound and if properly used will provide the accurate feedback needed by all the professionals associated with basketball. The author hopes that his months of research at least revealed to you that there is much useful data hidden in the boxscores and career-statistics and that this data may be extracted and put to great use.